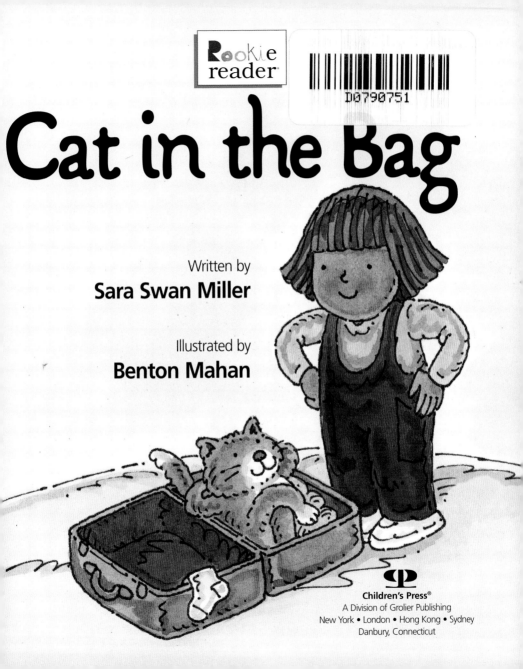

Rookie reader

D0790751

Cat in the Bag

Written by
Sara Swan Miller

Illustrated by
Benton Mahan

Children's Press®
A Division of Grolier Publishing
New York • London • Hong Kong • Sydney
Danbury, Connecticut

For Erin. Thanks for the cat!
—S. S. M.

To my daughters, Megan and Kailey. Forever my joy and inspiration.
—B. M.

Reading Consultants

Linda Cornwell
Coordinator of School Quality and Professional Improvement
(Indiana State Teachers Association)

Katharine A. Kane
Education Consultant
(Retired, San Diego County Office of Education and San Diego State University)

Library of Congress Cataloging-in-Publication Data

Miller, Sara Swan.
    Cat in the bag / by Sara Swan Miller ; illustrated by Benton Mahan.
      p. cm. — (Rookie reader)
    Summary: A child tries to pack for a trip, but the cat keeps jumping
into the suitcase.
    ISBN 0-516-22014-4 (lib. bdg.)   0-516-27292-6 (pbk.)
    [1. Cats—Fiction. 2. Luggage—Packing—Fiction. 3. Travel—Fiction.]
I. Mahan, Ben, ill. II. Title. III. Series.
PZ7.M63344 Cat 2001
[E]—dc21
                                    00-038426

Are you taking a trip?

What will you pack?

One sweater, one jacket,
one scarf, one hat.

No, no!
Not the CAT!

Two shirts, two shoes,
three pants, three caps.

Some socks—four pair.
And yes, underwear!

But NO CATS!
Get out of there!

Five books, six games,
a ball, a toy train.

Some paper, a pen,

and crayons . . .
one, two, three, four, five,
six, seven, eight, nine, ten!

A brush, shampoo,

and the cat?

Oh, okay . . .

you come, too!

Word List (56 words)

a	four	pair	ten
and	games	pants	the
are	get	paper	there
ball	hat	pen	three
books	jacket	scarf	too
brush	nine	seven	toy
but	no	shampoo	train
caps	not	shirts	trip
cat	of	shoes	two
cats	oh	six	underwear
come	okay	socks	what
crayons	one	some	will
eight	out	sweater	yes
five	pack	taking	you

About the Author

Sara Swan Miller has enjoyed working with children all her life, first as a Montessori nursery school teacher and later as an outdoor environmental educator at the Mohonk Preserve in New Paltz, New York. She has two children, both safely grown up. She has written more than thirty books, including *Three Stories You Can Read to Your Dog*, *Piggy in the Parlor and Other Tales*, and *Better than TV*. She has also written many books on animals for Children's Press and Franklin Watts.

About the Illustrator

Benton Mahan lives with his wife Anna on a farm in rural Ohio near the farm where he was raised. He teaches at the Columbus College of Art and Design in Columbus, Ohio, and has his studio in his home. He has illustrated more than fifty children's books as well as greeting cards and magazines. His art has been chosen for several UNICEF cards. He also currently has work on display at the Gallery of Contemporary Art in Rome, Italy. Benton has two grown daughters. The drawings for the girl in this book were based on his daughter Kailey and her cat Teaser. Kailey and her sister Megan used to dress Teaser in doll clothes.